I'M JUST PHONING
TO CHASE MY INVOICE

The things you really need to know
when you set up in business

BRIAN JENNER

This book is dedicated to Matthew Male of
Future Perfect – the world's most formidable
English grammarian.
(www.future-perfect.co.uk)

Published by BomoBooks 2009
Telephone: 01202 551257
Email: info@chasingmyinvoice.co.uk

ISBN: 978-0-9563226-0-9

Design and typesetting by Goldust Design
Cover photographs by Philip Hartley

To find out more about self-employment
and to buy more copies of this book visit:

www.chasingmyinvoice.co.uk

INTRODUCTION

For ten years I've lived as an entrepreneur. Imagine any romantic idea, any pleasant illusion, any misconception about business, I've had it, and I've suffered the consequences. But, I'm still here. I'm still trading, and I do what I love doing, rather than enduring the limitations of a 9-5 job.

If you're already in business, this book identifies some of the dilemmas and offers some practical suggestions to inspire you to solve problems. If you're about to start your business, this book provides a short and amusing guide to some of the pitfalls.

I work as a speechwriter, which is quite an unusual vocation. I help other people say things in an entertaining way. There are plenty of books listing the dry procedures you have to go through to start up a new business. This book describes some of the characters you come across, the emotions you feel and the inevitable tribulations you face.

I've made some big misjudgements, but that doesn't mean I wasn't on the right track. There is often no other way to learn. Just remember what Eleanor Roosevelt once said: "Learn from the mistakes of others. You can't live long enough to make them all yourself."

Brian Jenner, July 2009

ACCOUNTS

....

Financial records are a spectacular extension of our ordinary senses. They are to business what the telescope and microscope are to science, what the lab tests and stethoscope are to doctors, what radars and maps are to navigators.

Michael Phillips, American businessman

Don't confuse any prejudices you might have towards accountants with your feelings towards accounts. Your accounts provide a beautiful picture of your business, and they repay hours of careful study and evaluation.

If I wanted to tell the story of my business during the past ten years, I can see it written down in perfect detail in my accounts. I can spot when I paid £1756.63 for an advert in the Thomsons Directory that led to no business. I can see when I paid an assistant far too much money. I can see that huge cheque I cashed when I did my first big corporate speechwriting job.

The restaurant map I published is in there. I can see the dozens of small cash payments I had to collect. I can see when I lost heart and slipped into debt and when I regained my confidence and returned to solvency.

The difference is that when I started out I just handed my accounts over to the accountant at the end of the year and hoped things would work out for the best. Now, I follow the story as it unfolds, and do my best to guide it towards a happy ending.

ACTION

Nothing will ever be attempted, if all possible objections must first be overcome.

Samuel Johnson, English writer

BUSINESS CARDS

When you take delivery of your first pristine business cards, it's a very exciting day. Don't ever let things get as bad as the man who handed me a business card and said: "The address is wrong and the telephone number is wrong, but the rest is okay."

BUSINESS PLAN

....

When you work on your own you still need a business plan. Why? Because it's so easy to forget what you're supposed to be doing. A business plan is a written statement reminding you of the purpose of your business with clear statements of what you plan to do and what outcomes you expect.

Write one for every project you undertake and have a general one with your objectives for the forthcoming year. If I am involving anyone else in the business plan I give them a copy.

Ask yourself questions like, what are you going to create? Why are your creating it? How are you going to make money? What are you going to do to start off? And most importantly how will you measure your success?

Does a business plan need to be a long document? No. Keep it short and to the point. If Winston Churchill wrote plans for the Second World War on the back of an envelope, you can write your business plan on a sheet of A4 paper. If your business plan isn't working out, create a new business plan.

CHARACTER

Reggie Perrin, the businessman in the BBC comedy, gets bored with his booming business and resolves to destroy it by employing people utterly unfitted to their roles. It doesn't work. The recruits turn out to be brilliant. Turnover and sales continue to rise. It's hard to judge character. After you have spent a few years taking on clients, employing people and using different suppliers, you learn how difficult it is.

When you meet someone for the first time, be aware of the small details of your interaction. This will give clues. What they do can be subtle or unsubtle, the skill is to spot its significance immediately. This is especially hard when you are focused on the attractive prospect of new business.

Katie sent me an email saying she wanted a speech. When I dialled the mobile number I got a message warning me I was phoning a premium line. I stopped the call and emailed her to say that she must have made some mistake. *I was the one making the mistake*. I wrote her a speech, which she never paid for. What would you expect from someone who had the cheek to get you to call her on a premium line?

When I was living in a shared house, we had a problem with the new flatmate, Alan. Food went missing in the fridge. When we confronted Alan about it, he said he had thought all the food was paid for out of the rent. He stopped doing it after that. A few months later, he lost his job and I employed him to do some work for me. Alan started using my computer to download illegal software and films. It was the fridge behaviour all over again.

CHARITY

When I started in business, I wanted to improve the world, work with people I liked and do good. I failed. I designed a website for my local church. Father Derek was exasperating to work for because it was almost impossible to get any information out of him, he never gave me any feedback on whether he was happy with what had been done, and he got the church administrator to query one of my invoices. The experience drove me to find a different congregation.

I became the governor of a local school. They needed someone to do some fundraising work for them, and I offered to do it for payment. I published a magazine and organised an auction. Working as a paid administrator among volunteers was hell. When Phyllis, an elderly churchwarden, heard I was getting paid, she approached me menacingly for a charitable donation. It was as if she expected me to give it all back on the spot.

If I want to improve the world, I now do it in my own

time. I don't expect to get paid for it. I choose to work with companies and individuals with plenty of money to pay my bills. They are more likely to understand how business works and they are more likely to appreciate good work.

A few years later I read an article by Sir Christopher Bland in the *Financial Times*, which gave an insight into why the values of businesses and good causes are sometimes at odds. He said: "I spent seven years as a management consultant, and I formulated what I modestly called Bland's Law: that the amount of back-biting, in-fighting and general skulduggery in an organisation is in direct proportion to the nobility of its goals. The worst behaviour I found was in a home for handicapped children in north London, closely followed by a large teaching hospital. Compared with that, Shell, ICI and British American Tobacco were relatively well behaved."

CLUTTER

Beware clutter. Clutter can take many forms: the clutter that obstructs workspace, the clutter that fills up days and the clutter that we have in our minds. Clutter can appear as too many emails in our inbox, too many papers on the floor or a backlog of accounts and receipts, which have not been filed away.

Mary is a highly talented interior designer. She has a friend called Sally and every day she drives several miles to walk Sally's dog. This would be fine, were Mary running a successful business, but she is not. She struggles to pay her bills. She doesn't take any money for petrol from Sally and she uses up a big chunk of time in the day fetching, walking and returning the dog. She makes her emotional attachment to the dog her priority, rather than her own financial welfare. Sadly, it's almost impossible to point out another person's clutter to them.

Only when we straighten out our business affairs, does the absurdity of what we have been doing become apparent. When I was worrying about money, I seemed to labour all week for little reward. When my business prospered, I charged more, I worked less and I had plenty of time for other activities.

COLLECTION

....

The two most beautiful words in the English language are 'cheque enclosed'.

Dorothy Parker, American writer

Here is a problem. At what point in the transaction are you going to get the money from the customer?

Contemplating my unpaid invoices used to cause me great frustration. I remember watching the scene in the film *Goodfellas* when two gangsters dangle a debt-ridden Florida gambler over a lion cage at the Lowry Park Zoo in Tampa. I thought I'd like to do that to some of my clients.

I sold advertising on a map, listing local restaurants. I was not confident that I would sell enough advertising to make the project happen, when I started out. I got the restaurants to fill in a form requesting the advertising they wanted. When the map was published, I had to go round to the restaurants again to collect the money.

I'd get to the restaurant and Salvatore had a day off, Alphonse was too busy to speak to me, and Mr Ahmed couldn't raise a cheque that day. Even when they saw my beautiful map, they grumbled about the colours or the general lack of response. That's what restaurant owners are like. I ended up having to persuade them several times over of the excellent value I was giving them.

When I first started writing speeches, I wasn't clear how I should collect my money. I issued invoices. Having worked hard to create an excellent speech, I would then have to devote time to chasing my money.

Gradually, I woke up to what I was doing wrong. Now, I send over the speech after I have been paid. I request a bank transfer or I use Paypal. If a business does request an invoice, I ask for payment within seven or fourteen days. (Something I learned from working with other suppliers.) As a result, I no longer have dreams of treating my clients like feckless gamblers in *Goodfellas*.

COMPETITION

My gym buddy, John, is a photographer with a gloomy disposition. He's dispirited by the arrival of digital photography, which means any Tom, Dick or Harry can call himself a photographer. Put 'Photographer Bournemouth' into Google, he tells me, and you get over 300,000 entries.

The poet Tennyson wrote: "I must lose myself in action, lest I wither in despair." It's important to pay attention to what the competition is doing, but don't fret about it.

CONTRACTS

Put all your business agreements in writing. You don't need a lawyer to draft a contract. My aunt had a buffet for her 50th birthday. She called up the catering company and specified the things she wanted, which included healthy food: no sausage rolls, pasties or vol-au-vents.

When it came to her party night, the caterers arrived with sausage rolls, pasties and vol-au-vents. By then it was too late to do anything about it.

On the following day, she went ballistic and told them she wasn't going to pay the £600 bill. Still, she couldn't be sure of her position. They could take her to the small claims court. If she had sent an email or a letter to the caterers detailing her requirements, they would have been powerless to charge her.

COURAGE

One definition of an entrepreneur is a person who doesn't have a job. When I first expressed the idea of setting out on my own, I remained attached to the idea of having the security of a job.

I had a day off midweek and I was sitting in a down-market café with an American friend in Shepherd's Bush. He said to me: "Look at these people. They don't have jobs. They still survive. You don't need a job to survive."

COURTESY

A Chinese proverb states: 'A man without a smiling face must not open a shop.' It helps to be a friendly and pleasant person if you're selling to people, but learn how to put the curt into courtesy.

I promise only what I deliver. If I'm not careful, clients

will come back to demand endless amendments to a speech. I met Melissa, whose husband, Jonathan, is a plasterer. She told me he was incredibly obliging towards his clients. If asked, he would make further alterations to a job, even after it was signed off. Jonathan obeyed the whims of fussy old ladies and he had clients owing him money and he wasn't doing anything about it. Jonathan was 'too nice'. Melissa felt angry and frustrated on his behalf.

CREATIVITY

My mother is an avid Bible reader. Whenever we had a supply problem in the family which didn't have an obvious solution, she would declare: "What hast thou in the house?"

This reference goes back to the story of Elisha and the Widow's Oil. A mother has creditors at the door wanting to take away her two sons and keep them as slaves because she can't pay a debt. Elisha says to the widow: "What hast thou in the house?" The widow replies nothing except for a jar of oil.

She was told to get some empty pots from the neighbours and start pouring out the oil. They kept bringing the pots and she kept pouring out the oil. Then he told her to sell the oil to cover the debts and look after themselves.

This is a great lesson in creativity. When I fear that I might have to invest in new equipment or buy extra things to finish a job, I ask myself what do I have already available to me that can solve this problem?

I met Graham who runs an international telemarketing service with offices all over the world. He told me that, when he started, he had seven people working in the family home using makeshift telephone headsets made out of coat hangers. Graham didn't spend any money on getting smart equipment or office space until he could be certain that the new business was viable.

The most absurd example of how not to do this was Dmitri. Dmitri needed to produce flyers to promote his courses at an airbrush paint studio. He invested in a colour photocopier for £6,000. He was then able to produce some excellent colour flyers. Only he realised later that he could get the print shop across the road to print several hundred flyers for £30.

CUSTOMER CHOICE

A man was walking through a market place, and he bumped into a stall selling dinner plates and knocked them all over. He apologised to the trader and helped him put everything back. Some plates were selling for £2 and others were £3. The man said to the trader: "Some of these plates are £2 and some are £3, but I can't tell the difference."

The market trader said: "It doesn't really matter. Some customers just like to pay a premium for things."

DECISIONS

What's the difference between a sensible decision and an impulsive one? There is a technique called the 'Benjamin Franklin Close' that is used by salesmen to persuade a hesitant customer to make a purchase.

Take a plain piece of paper, and draw a line down the middle. On one side, write 'yes', on the other side you write 'no'. Then make a numbered list of all the reasons for taking the decision, and then another list of all the reasons for not taking the decision. Then weigh them in the balance.

A salesman will ask you to do this, because he will be helping you fill in the 'yes' column. He will do his best to overcome any objections in the 'no' column. When you have drawn up your lists, wait for several days. See if you still feel driven to take the decision. Charles Darwin used the technique to work out whether he should get married or not. Under 'Not marry' he jotted down: 'Not forced to visit relatives. Freedom to go where one liked.' Under 'Marry' he noted: 'Children (if it please God)' and, 'Constant companion (and friend in old age) who will feel interested in one.' He weighed up the arguments, for and against, and made up his mind to get married.

DIFFICULT PERSONALITIES

I worked as a freelance journalist for Martin, a magazine publisher. He was always late making payments. He got in the habit of commissioning work, but he would pay for the previous piece of work only when he had received the new article. Since money was tight, I believed that I had to continue working for Martin because it was income.

One day, Martin's assistant called me up in a panic. They needed my article within a few hours because the deadline had been brought forward. I was busy doing other work. It was hard decision to make, but I just said: "No". I lost my previous payment and I never spoke to him again. The best way to deal with people like Martin is to give them a wide berth.

DO IT YOURSELF

In an ideal world, we do those things that we are best at, and employ others to do everything else. My colleague Matthew corrects people's English. If a business is publishing a website or a brochure, he will read through it and find any spelling mistakes, omissions or problems with grammar/syntax.

It's not a very expensive service, but when the budget is limited, all extra costs are unwelcome. On big jobs, I always use him, since there is nothing worse than printing an expensive glossy brochure and finding a couple of spelling mistakes.

When I'm writing just a few words, I'm tempted to rely on my own proofreading skills. I did this on a diary which I sent to the printers. 500 colour diaries came back listing the dates of the meetings for my creative networking group. The problem was I missed off the time of the meeting. It was infuriating.

Thankfully, I'm not the only one. A government agency was in the habit of using Matthew for big jobs. One year, it printed a Christmas card. Naturally, in the office, they thought they would not employ a proofreader to check just two words.

Those two words were 'Season's Greetings'. When the card came back from the printers and had been sent out to thousands, somebody realised that they had missed off the apostrophe. They had to print them again and apologise, at a cost of around £300,000. Given that my friend charged seven pence per word, for the sake of 14 pence, it was a costly mistake.

EMPLOYING PEOPLE

If you have a business that can function without employees, don't have any. I offered two students work experience with different results.

One evening, an email dropped into my inbox from a student in Austria. Ania was looking for work experience in London. I was doing well and I had some projects that could do with some assistance, so I said yes. I was considerate. I advised her on a place to stay. I met her at the station. I took her out for a meal. I wanted to do things properly – not how I had been treated as an employee. I even offered to pay her token wages.

Ania came to work. I wrote down the tasks she had to do. But it soon became apparent she had no interest in doing them. She groaned and put her feet on the table. After a few days, it was impossible. I told her that I couldn't continue to employ her. She then told me that the reason she wanted to be in London was to be with her boyfriend. Getting work experience was just a pretext to persuade her mother to let her come over.

A few weeks later, I got another call, from Sarah, a student who had to do a placement as part of her course. I asked her what skills she had and what sort of tasks she wanted to do. I was brusque. She would have to supply her own laptop, she would have to do what I requested, and there was no prospect of a job at the end of it. She listened to what I had to say and still wanted to go ahead. Sarah did some excellent work and ended up getting a full-time job through one of my business contacts.

ENQUIRIES

Working on your own means you combine many roles: sales, marketing, accounts, IT, reception and much more. I'm often deeply immersed in writing a speech, when a potential client calls me up to make an enquiry about my services. It can be hard to get my brain in gear, and on occasions, I have said something silly or made a foolish quote for a job.

I resolved this problem by printing an 'enquiry sheet'. I have a printed sheet of A4 with blanks for the name of the client, the telephone number, the email, what type of speech they want and when they want to deliver it. So, when I get a potential customer on the telephone, I interrupt the caller and say: "Can you hang on for a second while I fetch one of my enquiry forms?"

By going through this process, I achieve three things.

1. I sound as if I am professional and in control.

2. I give myself time to think about how I am going to deal with this enquiry.

3. By giving me this information, the client is becoming more involved in the transaction. It becomes harder to turn around and say: "Actually, I'm going to get some other quotes before I decide whether to go with you."

EXPENSIVE

I commissioned work from Peter, a graphic designer based in the Manchester area. Peter had done excellent work for a friend of mine. I was a bit nervous about using him because of his fees. We built up a relationship working on the phone, by email and by post.

Paying Peter's invoices usually hurts a bit. But the smart look generates more clients and better quality business for me. There are other benefits. I can observe how he charges for his time and how he presents himself. It gives me ideas on how to sharpen up my act and get the proper reward for my services.

FAILURE

Henry, a business adviser, provoked silent awe in a seminar one day when he announced that: "There are three reasons why a business fails:

1. The owners have a business and they don't know what the purpose is.

2. The owners have a business and they are prevented from fulfilling its purpose because of external circumstances.

3. The owners know what the purpose is, but they're not doing it."

FEEDBACK

It's often tempting to try to straighten out other people's business problems. If you're not being paid to do so, it can be a big mistake. I got into the habit of watching videos posted on the website of a speaker bureau. One day I discovered that the website wasn't working, so I emailed Eric, the owner of the business and pointed this out. Eric emailed me back to say it *was* working properly. I checked again, and I couldn't get it to function.

A month or so later I was invited along to an event organised by the speaker bureau. There were many unsatisfactory elements to the day, and I decided to share them with Eric, since he had given me a free ticket. I pointed that we had no clear directions where to go and we were networking in pitch darkness. I explained how he could improve the way the speakers were introduced. I ended by suggesting a drink, as we were in complementary businesses.

A few minutes later I got a phone call from Eric. He launched into a tirade of foul-mouthed abuse. Just to make sure I got the message he followed this up with an abusive email saying that he didn't want to have a drink with me, or anybody who ever knew me.

What conclusion did I draw? Eric had a problem dealing with bad news. I set myself up as the target of his wrath and frustration. If a service is flawed, the kindest thing you can do is avoid using it again.

FINANCIAL LITERACY

....

It is better to have a permanent income than to be fascinating.

Oscar Wilde, Irish writer

For the time I have been in business, I have had good years and bad years. It didn't matter very much because I was financially illiterate. I was not aware of how to manage my personal finances, so all the money I earned, I spent. I just assumed that the way I managed my money was the only way. Only after years of struggling to pay my taxes and manage my money did I start reading about money and the proper way to handle it.

There are two books I recommend, *Your Money or Your Life* by Joe Dominguez and Vicki Robin and *How to Get Out of Debt, Stay Out of Debt, and Live Prosperously* by Jerrold Mundis. They explain the basics of good money management.

FLATTERY

Don't try to teach pigs to sing. Why not? Two reasons, 1) Pigs can't sing and 2) It annoys the pig.

Chinese Proverb

For a time my marketing strategy was to identify companies and organisations that were doing things badly, and suggest that I could be the man to fix them.

I identified a top politician who was delivering poor speeches. I decided to edit one of his speeches, showing how I could dramatically improve his style. It didn't work. So I changed tactic. I targeted individuals who were already giving brilliant speeches. My new line was: "You already give excellent speeches. Working with the theory that an individual who already delivers excellent speeches is best able to appreciate the value of a good speechwriter, I thought I would get in touch."

This was immediately successful. If a company or organisation is doing something badly, it's because they don't care, or don't know how it can be done well. Far better to approach organisations that are flourishing and producing excellent products, because they understand what quality is.

FREE

....

People that pay for things never complain. It's the guy you give something to that you can't please.

Will Rogers, American comedian

Be wary of any product or service that is free. Business is a wonderful concept. You use your intelligence and discretion to spend money in a way that will generate more money.

FRIENDS

My mother's side of the family knew Mr Quayle, a shoe-maker, who was a very shrewd businessman. His byword was: 'You don't have friends in business.'

Some customers knew Mr Quayle well. They would come to his shop and have no money to pay for their shoes. They would ask if they could pay later. Mr Quayle put the shoes back under the counter.

What did Mr Quayle mean? He meant that if he repaired shoes for friends and didn't insist on payment, he rapidly wouldn't have a business. You can't allow your friends to take advantage of you. I once saw a notice on a pub wall: 'Eat and drink with family and friends, but do business with strangers.'

GESTURES

A small gesture can have a big impact. Roy, a busi-nessman from the Midlands, asked me to write a speech for his wife's 50th birthday. I interviewed him. He was obviously a very rich man. He got the speech. I wasn't sure whether he liked it or not.

Roy called me back and said he was very happy with

it and he was sending me my money "and an extra £50 from my wife". I nearly fell off my chair with shock. If Roy ever gets in touch again, I'll drop everything to work for him.

GOOD IDEAS

....

The trouble is, if you don't risk anything, you risk even more.

Erica Jong, American writer

Dreaming up products and services is an almost mystical process. There is no shortage of good ideas. The trick is to put them into practice. You can never really know what will sell. So what possible means can you use to evaluate an idea? Do you feel comfortable with it? Are you looking forward to doing it? Are you willing to make sacrifices? There are no cast iron ways to determine whether an idea is worth pursuing or not, but you can ask yourself, does the idea have:

1. Place?

Can you imagine where it will happen? Is there a venue or a space where you can see it working? A Greek mathematician, Pappus of Alexandria, once said: "Let us start with what is being sought and assume we have already found it."

2. Direction?

Are there indications that you are part of an identifiable trend? Can you point to evidence that people will desire your product or service because it's working in other places?

3. Velocity?

You need to work very hard to get a new idea off the ground. Having done the hard work, it should acquire some momentum. Are you hitting objections at every step? If an idea stubbornly refuses to take off, it may be because it's ahead of its time or it may be because it's not a good idea.

GOVERNMENT

Some people make the understandable mistake that government is there to help the small business person. It's true, if you want to set up in business, you may be entitled to benefits. When I first started out, I had to claim unemployment benefit for six months to be entitled to join the Prince's Trust business scheme. During that time, I had small amounts of money coming in that I had to declare.

This caused chaos. As soon as I became entitled to claim housing benefit, I would receive a letter that it was going to be cut off again because I was earning too much. I went to my business adviser, David, and told him of my woes trying to get my housing benefit. "Oh, you must create a big fuss," he said. "The squeakiest wheel gets the oil."

Then he explained how another one of his clients had a similar problem getting her benefit. "They refused to pay her, so she handcuffed herself to the railings outside the benefit office, until they agreed to pay up."

"And do you know," David said, "she influenced government policy. From then on, a decree went out that all housing benefit centres should remove any railings outside of their offices."

HOLIDAYS

Some self-employed people say: "I can't afford to go on holiday. What if I got a really good piece of business while I was away?" Really, the statement should be turned around. If you can't take a holiday, maybe your business is not prospering as it ought to. You need to take action to do something about it.

I can identify a clear moment in the improvement of my fortunes. I was invited to Washington DC to give a lecture to a conference of American speechwriters. I treated myself to five days in New York: the first proper holiday I had had in years. It was a rejuvenating experience.

HOPELESS CAUSES

Hopeless causes can become very attractive. I ran a community news website in London. I wanted to solve the problems of the neighbourhood. The site attracted lots of attention and I built it into a popular service, with one problem, it hardly made any money. In fact, money I made from other sources, I ploughed back into this project.

It did bring me a small income, and most people will concede that it takes time for a business to mature and make a good profit. However, over time, the sole good reason for continuing with the website was because I had already invested so much time and money creating it. The less clear it was how I would ever make any money out of it, the more keen I was to spend money promoting the service.

To become an effective business person, the most important skill may not be setting something up, it may be the ability to recognise when the most profitable course is to close something down. The lesson I learned was that I need ways to protect myself against my own reluctance to admit defeat.

Later, when I moved to Bournemouth, I decided to set up a creative business networking group. When I wrote the business plan, I gave myself a deadline. I planned three evenings as market research. If I could host three busy and vibrant evenings and cover my costs, it would be deemed a success and I would carry on. If hardly anyone showed up, I would stop. One way of protecting myself from pursuing a hopeless cause was to define how I would distinguish success from failure.

HUMILITY

With the advent of the World Wide Web, it's tempting to create an image that you have dozens of employees or that you are occupying enormous offices; actually, it's you with your laptop and your mobile phone, sitting in a poky study.

I called myself Tarsus Communications. We did websites, brochures, publishing, copywriting, public speaking training, consulting etc, etc. It took me ten years to wake up to what I do best: Brian Jenner trading as The Speechwriter. Once I had accepted that, a number of other ideas occurred to me as income streams, writing books, giving lectures and organising conferences.

ILLUSIONS

....

When we get the bracing idea to set up a new business, there is the rather beguiling fantasy that we might be about to set up the next Google, or a mighty brand like Marks & Spencer. Actually most businesses only last a few years, some last a decade, it's extraordinary if a firm lasts for a lifetime. A business is just a vehicle to manage an activity that makes money. If we make a living from it for a few years, that's something to be grateful for.

INVERSION

....

Whenever you face a difficult business problem, write down what you want to avoid. I use it in my speech-writing. Let's say a successful man is invited back to his old school to do a speech on how to be successful in life. He could express some worthy and noble sentiments. But it might be more entertaining and illuminating to analyse why others have not prospered. How do people ruin their potential and let themselves down? Invert problems, it gives you a fresh perspective.

INVOICING

My hobby is salsa dancing. When you have a bit of experience, you realise that to ask a woman point blank: "Would you like to dance with me?" is a very dangerous thing to do. It's so easy for her to just say: "No." What you do is you walk past her, turn, and hold your hand out gracefully. It makes it far harder for her to say no.

I did some work for a big insurance company. The company had commissioned me to create a map of the local area. Alice, a junior member of staff, asked me to make amendments to the map. So I phoned up and said that these amendments would require extra work. I also asked if I could add £150 to the bill. Alice said: "No." I should have just added the extra charge to the invoice.

KAMIKAZE ANTICS

A Zen student once asked his teacher: "Master, what is enlightenment?" The master replied: "When hungry, eat. When tired, sleep." I've noticed that when I have got into a bad state, exhibiting self-destructive tendencies, I haven't been eating properly, or I have been working too hard. Entrepreneurs tend to have lots of energy, so when their plans are frustrated, they can sink into irrational despair. By temperament, entrepreneurs can be very creative, and very self-destructive.

I heard a presentation from a businessman who said starting up his enterprise gave him the same satisfaction as building a Lego tower when he was four years old. When things went wrong, destroying the business gave him the same satisfaction as kicking a Lego tower over when he was four years old.

When you run into difficulties ask yourself a series of questions, are you eating properly? Are you exercising? Are you sleeping normally? Are you angry about something? Have you been working too hard?

The answers to these questions are often very revealing. If you're suffering, your judgement is impaired. You'll make reckless decisions and do stupid things. By dealing with these prosaic matters, you can begin to get your sanity back.

I start each day by weighing up my options for lunch. It's an exercise that reminds me that I always have choices.

LEGAL ACTION

I remember reading the obituary of a colourful judge in the *Daily Telegraph*. His advice was, never go to law, swallow your pride and settle. Conflict absorbs so much of your energy if you work on your own that unless you can solve your problem by a quick visit to the small claims court, just put the loss down to experience and move on.

LIMITED COMPANY VERSUS SOLE TRADER

Matthew, the grammarian, graphically illustrated to me the advantage of being a limited company. He corrected the text of a poster which was to appear on hoardings all over London. In the process of sending the text to be printed, one mistake reappeared.

The posters went up all over London costing many thousands of pounds. The campaign then had to be abandoned, when the mistake was discovered. The company which had commissioned the advertising campaign was then seeking to recoup its losses, by identifying the person liable for the error.

Luckily, Matthew could prove he had submitted the correction. Otherwise, as a sole trader, he could have lost his house, his car and his life savings. He then decided to become a limited company. If something like this happened again, and it could be proven that he was at fault, he would be able to protect his personal assets by winding up his company.

LONELINESS

....

In the film *Zulu*, there is a moment when the British troops at Rorke's Drift know they are going to be attacked by an overwhelming force of Zulu warriors. And there is a discussion between the two British officers Chard and Bromhead as to who will take command. Chard was commissioned before Bromhead, so he takes control.

Then a deputation of British irregular cavalry ride by on horseback and Lt Chard begs them to stay to help them defend the garrison. They need the extra men. But the irregular cavalry just ride off into the distance.

Lt Chard complains: "You didn't say a word to help, Bromhead." Lt Bromhead replies: "Oh, when you're in command, old boy, you're on your own. The first lesson the general, my grandfather, taught me."

When you're running your own business, you're on your own. Loneliness can be a big problem. It's hard making decisions that you will be directly responsible for. It's hard to explain to other people what you do. Some family members think I sit at home all day doing nothing.

You will also experience envy and anger. Lots of people desire to do their own thing, but they lack the courage to do so. They want you to fail because it would reassure them that it is not possible.

MAD AMBITION

....

What does a speechwriter do? I provide a script for a client to read out on an important occasion. Sometimes, people get the wrong end of the stick. For example, the man who sent me an email, phoned me up and called me on my mobile all within a few minutes of each other at around midday on a Sunday. He was going to be a best man. He wanted a fantastic speech. He wanted it to be incredibly funny (there would be media people there). I tried to dampen down his expectations a bit. I couldn't turn him into Jonathan Ross.

"How much would you charge me for the speech?"

I said I would charge him my standard rate.

"Well, that doesn't sound right, for a really excellent speech, I would be willing to pay three times that."

"Right," I said. "Well, if you don't like the material, I can rewrite it for you and charge you more."

He sent me a cheque for my standard rate and I wrote him the speech. I never heard back from him. Whether he liked it or not, or whether he delivered it or not, wasn't really the issue. He really wanted something money couldn't buy. The fact that he didn't respect normal working hours was a clue that he was a client with unrealistic expectations.

MENTORS

I was once at an awards ceremony for social entrepreneurs. An MP announced that one of the prizes was a consultation with a blue-chip management consultancy firm. They would sit down with the winners and advise them on how to develop their idea. "And if your business can survive that," he said, "it may well go on to great things."

Consultants may be highly-paid and work in smart offices but they don't have a monopoly on wisdom. We have friends we admire, and they give us their advice. Accountants and lawyers have great ideas, too. Often, little me feels intimidated by brands and people with status. I feel obliged to do as they say.

My feeling now is that, I'm in charge. I have to evaluate advice for myself. I have confidence in my own ability to make decisions and ignore 'experts' if necessary.

MOTION

If things aren't getting any better, they're often getting worse. The danger of not making efforts to generate new business is that you will start surviving on less and less income. The function of persistent marketing is not just to make sales, but rather to focus the mind on where you're heading and how you're going to get there. As the founder of Tesco, Jack Cohen once put it: "You can't do business sitting on your arse."

MOTIVATION

Of all the time-management theories in the world, it's hard to beat Granny's Law. Granny's Law states: Eat your carrots before your dessert.

NEEDS

Just because you face a particular problem doesn't mean it makes a good idea for a business. My friend Alex didn't have a girlfriend. He thought, quite rightly, that many men find it very difficult to find a girlfriend. So, he set up a singles' night. He booked a venue and sold tickets.

Alex's first problem was that he couldn't balance the men and the women. On the opening night, he had 80 women and only ten men. Then on the second night he had 120 men and ten women. Since the men had paid £5 each to get in, they were very angry. The next morning Alex had a death threat on his answerphone.

The amount of money he made out of the project was negligible, though he did manage to have a brief relationship with one of the ladies who attended one of his events. It broke up after one week. Two months later, he was informed that he was the father of the child this lady was expecting. Alex disputed paternity, but when he had the test, he was proved to be the father. He decided to emigrate to Australia.

Alex would have been better off spending money on other dating agencies, and then once he had found a girlfriend, he could devise his own dating concept. Alternatively, he could have set up a gay singles' club. At least then he would not have confused his own needs with the needs of his customers.

NEGOTIATION

When you're negotiating a price, a client will sometimes say: "If it goes well I might have more business for you later in the year."

Funnily enough, the business rarely materialises. On one particular occasion, a client dangled an opportunity in front of me: "I've got a brochure and a website that needs writing soon."

So what? I am a specialist speechwriter. I know exactly how to charge as a speechwriter, I know how it's done and how to manage customers' expectations. I don't know how to charge for web copywriting. In my small business, I need jam today. Jam tomorrow is no good.

Similarly, someone representing a 'good cause' may say, if you do this free, it might lead to other offers of work. In my experience, it definitely does lead to other offers of work – more requests to do work for no payment.

NEPOTISM

Nepotism may not be such a bad thing after all. The person who successfully starts and runs a small business usually had either a parent or a close relative who had a business. If you're trying to work out whether you've got the drive to set up a business, look for family connections.

NETWORKING

If you work on your own, you need to get out and socialise. (Birds of a feather flock together: when I gave up my day job, very rapidly my friendships with former work colleagues faded). You always need to be generating new business, and you need the mental stimulation of hearing about what other people are doing.

Networking for the sake of networking soon loses its appeal. I provide a highly specialised service to anyone in the English-speaking world who can afford to pay. I've discovered I'm unlikely to get much business in my home town.

Before you sign up for an event or join a group, work out your motivation for going along. Does the group share your abilities and aspirations? Are you going to make sales? If so, are you also prepared to make purchases? Does the setting reflect your brand values?

Whenever I do meet a person with whom I have something in common with, I suggest that we have a lunch every month. I find a regular long lunch with someone in a similar business provides me with inspiration, consolation and stability.

OLDEST PROFESSION

....

Prostitution provides two crude examples of qualities required in business.

The first is that prostitutes usually ask for their money up front for a good reason. They would have great difficulty getting the money after the transaction is over.

Secondly, Michael Phillips, in his book *Honest Business* tells a story about how prostitutes have incredible persistence. He observed a project to retrain street prostitutes. Most of these working women had an attention span of five minutes, if there was no danger or excitement around. They tried to retrain them as telephone switchboard operators, but sitting down all day didn't appeal to them. No matter how many times they were put in jail for prostitution they were always right back at work the same day they got out of prison.

PARTNERSHIP

According to the Prayer Book, there are three reasons to get married. First, to bring up children; secondly, to avoid sin. And thirdly, to keep each other company and care for each other when things go wrong. There isn't much in there about fun or romance. So, why do people choose go into business partnership together? It may be to avoid loneliness. It may be to combine skills. It may be to raise capital. Whatever the reason, be aware that the potential consequences of a business partnership that goes wrong. The tragedy of a bad partnership is the same tragedy as a bad marriage. The two parties often soldier on rather than face the consequence of divorce and everyone and everything involved is overcome by paralysis.

I know a brilliant cake-maker called Vincent, who is in business with a genial café proprietor, Louis. Five years ago, I suggested they get a website. They haven't done that yet. The tops of the teapots have broken, and rather than buy new teapots they cover the lids with saucers. The signage outside says they are open on a Sunday, but they are closed on a Sunday. One afternoon I was in the café and a woman came in selling a service. The proprietor said: "Oh it's nothing to do with me, you'll have to speak to the boss."

"Is your name Louis?"

"Yes."

"Well, I spoke to Vincent this morning who said that he wasn't the boss. I had to speak to Louis." It was embarrassing for everyone to overhear, but it said a great deal about the state of the business. The multimillionaire publisher, Felix Dennis, in his book *How to Get Rich*, points out that you don't get wealthy by sharing with a business partner the fruits of your own good ideas.

PRICING

People value what they pay for, and pay for what they value.

Thomas Szasz, American psychiatrist

You can learn something from the joke about how a good optician operates. He charges the client for the eye test and asks him to choose a frame. "That'll be £175," says the optician. If the client doesn't blink, he says: "and the lenses are £70". If the client still doesn't blink, he adds: "Each."

PUBLIC LIFE VERSUS PRIVATE LIFE

If you are the business, do your best to draw boundaries between your private life and your business life. The nature of bad habits is that they will gradually worsen over time. Here are five suggestions to help you to do that.

1. See the money in your business account as wine. See the money in your personal account as beer. Every month you need to draw a salary which turns wine into beer. Never mix up beer and wine because you will make yourself and the business sick.

2. Have one mobile phone for business use and another mobile phone for personal use. Give one number to friends and the other number to business contacts. When you finish work, switch off your business mobile phone. Do the same with email addresses. This makes it easier to evaluate the state of your business life and your personal life.

3. If you work from home, put everything that belongs to the business in one designated space. Take everything that doesn't belong to the business out of that designated space. If you start buying things for the business that don't go in the designated space, ask yourself why this is.

4. When you are evaluating your expenses, work out if they truly belong to the business or to you. Charge the business for every expense that it incurs. Do not fail to charge it for some things, and make up for it by putting through some dubious personal expenses. You're either stealing from yourself, or stealing from the business.

5. The proverb says that cobblers' children have no shoes. A highly talented individual often fails to apply expertise to personal problems. How does this apply to you?

PUBLIC SPEAKING

If you can stand up and make a 30 second presentation in front of a room of 100 people, explaining who you are and what product of service you supply, it's a very cheap and effective form of advertising.

If you have fears around speaking in public, Toastmasters International is a non-profit educational organisation that operates clubs worldwide for the purpose of helping members improve their communication, public speaking and leadership skills. Find your local club and you will have opportunities to practise business presentations and meet a supportive group of people, many of whom run their own businesses.

PURPOSE

Henry, a rather fierce business adviser, once asked me: "What is the purpose of Brian Jenner?"

I was floored by the question for a while. As a way of helping me formulate a better response, Henry said that he had expressed a desire to his sister to get a dog. She said that would be fine, but he should work out what the purpose of the dog would be. If the dog knew what its purpose was, let's say to exercise the owner, to guard the house or to be a pet for the children, it would be happy.

RESPONSE

John has given up his day job to become a web designer. He's launched a website promoting his services. After two weeks he's getting a bit jumpy because he has had no response. He's made a projection that he will be able to earn what he was earning in work within the first year. I discussed John's expectations with a friend. We were amazed at his impatience. One of the hardest things to endure for someone new to self-employment is the fact that there can be days or weeks when the telephone doesn't ring.

When I was promoting my creative business group, I gave a young woman who worked in the Post Office one of my flyers. Two years later when I was buying some stamps, she said she wanted to find out more about it. That evening she went along. Two years between doing the promotion and getting some business. That's not unusual.

RESTAURANTS

If you want to study how business works, there are few more fascinating case-studies than restaurants. You see evidence of broken dreams on every high street in Britain. It's a poignant sight. A pile of post on the floor, dirty windows and chaos, where there was once smart tablecloths and pretty waitresses. A dream has died. Someone put huge amounts of money and effort into creating an exciting new concept and now there's an aggressive note from bailiffs in the window, or a 'To Let' sign above the door.

One of the most successful restaurants in London I knew was downmarket – one internet reviewer said he had eaten the worst meal of his life there. They served semi-defrosted pizzas, chicken and chips or spaghetti bolognese. The staff were unhelpful. To see the chef, you wouldn't trust him with your drains, let alone your prawn cocktail. But it was always busy. Why? Because if you're a tourist in a foreign town, you want some-where simple and inexpensive. Moderate grubbiness is reassuring.

The lesson to learn from restaurants is that there are many factors determining their success. The key to creating a popular restaurant may have nothing to do with the food. It could be the location. Every town has its restaurant graveyard. A row of shops which is irre-sistible to naïve entrepreneurs. They ignore the fact that about six restaurants have failed in the same spot within recent memory. Oh no. Build it and they will come.

SALES

....

You can learn a lot about sales from beggars and con-artists. One lunchtime, I was on my way to buy some sandwiches in the local supermarket. A man stopped me and asked me if I was local. I was local. I was local and proud of it. I edited the local community website.

He explained that he was a coach driver and his coach had broken down. He pointed to the coach that was parked in the street outside my house.

"I need money for a new belt driver. Have you got any change? I'll deliver it back to you in half-an-hour – straight to your house, with a fiver on top."

I only had two ten pound notes in my wallet, which he saw. "Look," he said, "I really need £17.99 for this belt."

I gave him £20. I told him number 42, the bell marked Jenner.

"I'll remember." he said.

"What's your name?" I asked, "Michael Bentley," he replied.

He looked me in the eye and shook me by the hand. "It's a pleasure to do business with you." he said.

I headed for the supermarket. Suddenly I had a queasy sense that something was wrong. I bought my sandwiches and ran back home. To my relief, the coach was still parked outside my flat. I jumped on the coach.

"Have you broken down?"

"Yes" said the driver. "Do you have another driver called Michael Bentley?" "No."

Why did I give Mr Bentley the money? I analysed my impulses. First, he was charming and he made me feel good about myself. Secondly, he pointed to physical evidence that made his case convincing (full marks for ingenuity on his part: he saw the coach and saw an opportunity to spin a yarn); thirdly, he appealed to my self-interest, by promising to return the money with £5 on top.

At that time, I was involved with selling advertising for a local brochure. I applied those three techniques. I was charming. I pointed to the new office development and I reassured them it would be the only way to advertise their services to these new workers. The brochure was a success and I made a few thousand pounds.

Several years later, I had a beggar come up to me and use the line: "Do you speak English?" When I said that I did, his follow-up line was: "What a relief. So many people round here can't even speak English." He then asked me for some money for a cup of tea. I was impressed. He reminded me of the importance of a good sales hook.

SCRIPTS

I can't always trust myself when I'm put under pressure. If a salesman has worked hard, sometimes I feel that I ought to reward him with a sale.

As a speechwriter, I understand the value of rehearsing pre-prepared lines. One is: "I am sorry, but I have one of those impulsive disorders. I never make immediate purchases. I'm afraid I will not be able to make a decision now. But thank you for your presentation." It's off-the-wall enough to break the spell of any skilled salesman.

I occasionally get asked to speak in public by charities or voluntary groups. It can be very difficult to say no. I overheard a top designer say once: "I get asked to speak at events all the time, and I can't possibly do them all, so I have to charge, I'm afraid. My fee is £2,000." I wrote it down in my notebook for future use.

SECRETS

I got to know Bernard, a dentist. He was an affable chap. When I first when to his surgery he treated me with great courtesy. When it came to the bill, Bernard did a break-down of charges. So check-up fee, which was £40, he cut to £20 – "Because it's you." The cost of an X-ray, which was £60, he crossed through, and put £40. So when I left to go to see the receptionist and pay my bill, I thought: "What a great guy!"

A few months later Bernard asked me to do some marketing work for him. I sat in the office and saw the receipts for dental work. I noticed that he did these discounts for everyone. It was a bit of a disappointment. When I had a pretext to change to another dentist, I did so.

TALENT

....

Talent is cheaper than table salt. What separates the talented individual from the successful one is a lot of hard work.

Stephen King, American writer

TAXES

....

Robert Townsend in his book, *Up the Organization* says: "Ask yourself two questions every morning. 'Who do I least want to see? What do I least want to do?'

Chances are they'll be your top priority."

Doing your taxes falls into this category. Every year, millions of people submit their taxes on the weekend before the deadline. For year after year, I did not set money aside each month to pay my taxes. I was 'far too busy running my business'. Most years I had to dig deep into my reserves, raid my savings or borrow from family, until I had no more savings left.

I didn't want to think about money for eleven months of the year. All the administration of doing my accounts filled me with fear. Fear of the tax man is a great handicap for a business person. I now look at it like this. When I was in my 20s, I spent hundreds of hours learning to overcome my fear of public speaking. In my 30s, I spent several nights a week overcoming my fear of dancing. In my 40s, my priority is to allay all my fears about paying my taxes. I keep clear, orderly and accurate financial records and I keep track of my invoice due dates. From now on, I'm determined to look forward to my dealings with the Inland Revenue.

TERMS AND CONDITIONS

If you're running a business, you're inviting people to take part in a game, in which you write the rules. The terms and conditions are those rules.

I wanted to cancel my broadband supplier. I arranged to change to another supplier when my subscription ended. I still received a bill for three extra months. I read their terms and conditions and they stated clearly that you had to give them three months' notice if you want to disconnect the service. So I paid.

They also added on a £20 disconnection fee. I could find no reference to this on their terms and conditions. I wrote a letter refusing to pay, pointing out their omission. They kept sending invoices. I threatened to report them to Trading Standards. The invoices stopped coming.

I have to anticipate the problems that face me as the provider of a speechwriting service. A client may say: "I don't like the speech". What do I do then? I spell out exactly the service I am supplying in my terms and conditions. If I am confronted by a new problem, I deal with it, and then I edit my terms and conditions to clear up any misunderstanding in the future.

TESTIMONIALS

When you're selling your service, collecting testimonials from satisfied customers can be a powerful way to convince people that you're providing a good and reliable service.

I noticed that another speechwriter, Kevin, always collects about six testimonials a month. They all sound over the top, like, 'The audience was convulsed with laughter we even thought of calling an ambulance.'

This irritated me. I got feedback from some of my customers, but not all. How was he getting all these superlatives coming back? How was he getting so much business? I had a debate about this with my gym buddy, John, who is a photographer.

"Just make them up," he said.

I didn't feel comfortable about that. Later, John read through my testimonials. "One or two of them say that the client still had to do minor changes. That's no good. If I'm buying a speech from someone, I don't want to think that I'm going to have to do some extra work on it."

After thinking it over, I agreed with him.

Just be aware that some businesses may well make up their own testimonials, and others get influential friends to say nice things about them. Actually, I find the best use of testimonials is to convince myself. If I'm having a bad day, or I'm in an argument with someone over some issue, it helps to get out my glowing testimonials to remind myself that I've done huge amounts of good work for others.

TIMING

Running a business gives you lots to complain about. People with a job get paid every month for showing up. If you run a business you have to find the work, satisfy the client and collect the payment. There are times when you have bills to pay and you're not getting paid. It's at these times you learn the meaning of the phrase, 'manna from heaven'.

Its origin repays study. God heard the children of Israel in the wilderness complaining that they were going hungry. So He gave them manna from heaven. There were rules about gathering the manna. It had to be collected and eaten within the same day. If they attempted to keep it until the following morning, it became infested with worms. The only day when they were allowed to store it was on the Sabbath day, because they had to rest. Miraculously, the worms took a rest on that day, too.

Business has a rhythm to it. Don't pay bills early, don't pay them late, pay them when they're due.

TROUBLE

The thoughts of others
Were light and fleeting,
Of lovers' meeting
Or luck or fame.
Mine were of trouble,
And mine were steady,
So I was ready
When trouble came.

A E Housman, from Horace

UNDERCHARGING

I got a phone call just before Christmas. Sergio wanted a very short birthday speech for his wife's 50th. I told him I had a minimum charge. He said that it was too much. I was just putting down the phone when he said: "How about you do it for just a bit less?"

I wasn't busy, so I gave in. I calculated that I could dash it off in no time at all and it would pay for a few extra Christmas presents.

I wrote the speech, and sent it off. Sergio called me back and started being incredibly demanding. When it was all done, he didn't even acknowledge the fact that I interrupted my Christmas period to finish the job. It was a lesson. Undercharging not only means you don't earn what you deserve, it brings many other problems, too.

VISIONS

....

Empty pockets never held anyone back. Only empty heads and empty hearts can do that.
Norman Vincent Peale, American cleric

I have a friend called Emer who I meet for coffee every now and again and she has an idea for an open-air cinema experience in Bournemouth. She would like to see a big screen on the beach, with hundreds of people watching it on a summer evening. It's something she has seen work very well in Dublin.

Every time I meet her, she brings it up. However, she's a full-time teacher. She says she has no time or money to make it happen. Lots of people have a dream of something they would like to do. What is the solution if you have no time or money to make your business idea work? The answer is *do* something. If I have a 'vision', I open a file on my computer and I start writing a business plan for the idea.

My dream is to set up a French Cultural Centre in Bournemouth. I would like it to have a pâtisserie on the ground floor, a theatre on the second floor (with Moulin Rouge-style can-can girls appearing every evening) and a literary salon on the top floor, with French films and books available. Every now and again, more details pop into my head. I would like the music in the pâtisserie to be Françoise Hardy and Jacques Brel. I have also identified the building in which I would like this centre to be based. I write it all down on paper, despite the fact that I have no money to invest and no experience of the catering trade.

Writing my ideas down has three advantages. First, if I were to bump into a wealthy investor and he thought it was a brilliant idea, I could send that person a document with the plan on it the next day.

Secondly, by writing the ideas down, I stop them circling in my head. I get a clear sense of what the vision is and the obstacles I face to making it happen.

Thirdly, once the plan has been written down, I have a record of it. I can remind myself of my aspirations and plans at a later date. With time, I will get better at telling the difference between my mad ideas and my sane ones. At some level, maybe, by writing these ideas down, I act in a way that makes them more likely to happen.

WAIT

One of my heroes is General Kutuzov in Tolstoy's novel *War and Peace*. He had the task of defending Moscow from Napoleon's invasion. Rather than engaging with the enemy, Kutuzov retreated. He was concerned with saving the lives of his troops. And what did he do then? Nothing. His bywords were, 'Patience and Time'. He was patient because what he did have, according to Tolstoy, was a crystal-clear purpose.

"His actions – without the smallest deviation – were all directed to one and the same threefold end: (1) to brace all his strength for conflict with the French, (2) to defeat them, and (3) to drive them out of Russia, minimising as far as possible the sufferings of his people and of his army."

There is a paradox in the role of an entrepreneur. It doesn't always have to involve ceaseless activity. Once you have established a worthwhile goal, your actions, without the smallest deviation, must be focused on that goal. Patience often brings you more options. Don't take on unnecessary work and don't be busy just for the sake of being busy.

WORK FLOW

When you don't have a lot of work coming in, it can be tempting to linger over that work. Perhaps it's the fear that you'll be left with nothing to do. I have found that there is natural flow to work. Very often when you do sit down and finish the task in hand, the next piece comes in.

ZIHUATANEJO

Entrepreneurs are hopeful people. The film *The Shawshank Redemption* has a lot to say about hope. The main character, Andy Dufresne, is wrongly put in prison for the murder of his wife. Early on in his captivity he gets hold of a rock hammer. He tells everyone else that the hammer is to make small sculptures. Only at the end of the film do we discover the other purpose of the rock hammer. The story gives examples of many strategies to overcome seemingly impossible challenges.

Zihuatanejo is the place in Mexico where Andy Dufresne dreams of escaping to – it becomes a symbol of serenity, self-sufficiency and calm.

He describes it as a place with no memory. After ten

years of being in business on my own, I certainly wish to forget all my mistakes and misunderstandings, my disappointments and disasters. But a memory of them makes me the wiser businessman I am today. I am now content to provide a simple service which enables me to live well, maximising my income and minimising my stress.

For everyone who wants to take the route of running their own business, it helps to remember that we're not aiming for world domination, but Zihuatanejo – a place where we can be who we truly are, a place where we can enjoy work and leisure with the confidence that if we face sudden misfortune, we're smart enough and experienced enough to work ourselves out of it.

ABOUT THE AUTHOR

....

Brian Jenner works as a speechwriter and public speaker. He became self-employed in 1998 and was able to set up his own business, thanks to a loan from the Prince's Trust. He regularly gives talks to groups about the trials of working on his own in a creative business. He lives in Bournemouth, England.

Brian has started a blog collecting amusing stories about the experience of running a business. You can email him: **info@chasingmyinvoice.co.uk**